10 Minutes TO POWERFUL PRAYER

STORMIE OMARTIAN

HARVEST HOUSE PUBLISHERS

EUGENE, OREGON

Cover by Koechel Peterson and Associates, Minneapolis, Minnesota

10 MINUTES TO POWERFUL PRAYER
Copyright © 2010 by Stormie Omartian
Published by Harvest House Publishers
Eugene, Oregon 97402
www.harvesthousepublishers.com
ISBN 978-0-7369-2741-3

Printed in the United States of America

10 11 12 13 14 15 16 17 18 / VP-NI / 10 9 8 7 6 5 4 3 2 1

CONTENTS

> *Draw near to God
> and He will draw near to you.*
> JAMES 4:8

Answers to Your Questions Before You Even Ask

No, this is not a misguided attempt to reduce prayer to a formula. Nor am I trying to minimize the time we need to spend in prayer down to 10 minutes. And I certainly don't want to trivialize prayer to merely a "quick fix" for what ails us, or an "on-the-run" kind of praying so we can do our "duty" and get on to the many "more interesting" things we have to do in our lives.

First of all, I think prayer *is* interesting. In fact, I think it's fascinating. That's because prayer is communicating with God, and *He* is fascinating. And what He wants to do through your prayers and mine is amazing. When you understand that prayer is building a relationship with God and partnering with Him to see His will done in your life and situation—and in the lives and situations of others—you will find yourself wanting to pray as much as possible.

What I hope to do in this little book is give you a practical tool to help meet what I believe may be a need in your life. The reason I think you might have this need is because it is a need *I* have. If you're like me, there are things you pray about over and over—such as your health, the safety of family members, blessings over your work and finances, and guidance for decisions that have to be made. But it's hard to find time to pray about the many other important people and situations in your life. In addition to that, it is often easy to neglect such vital kinds of prayer as worship or confession. We don't mean to overlook these important areas of prayer focus and concerns, but there is always so much to pray about, and we can't think of everything.

Well, now *you* don't have to think of everything because *I* have provided the framework—the most important areas of prayer focus—that can help you have clear direction when you pray. While your most pressing needs are easy to focus on because they occupy your mind, this book will serve as a reminder of the other important things you don't want to forget.

Personally, I pray every day about many things, yet I still feel the need for a previously thought-out checklist that will prompt me to include certain people, situations, and issues in my life and in my world that I might not otherwise remember to pray about on my own. All of us can get busy in our day and feel that we don't have the time to pray adequately about certain things, so we end up not praying about them at all. I know. I've been there. In fact, I'm there now. I need this book too.

How This Book Works for You

Instead of having ten *chapters,* this book is divided into ten *areas of prayer focus.* Every paragraph in each of these ten areas of prayer focus is a complete thought and is, therefore, separated by a space from the others. That way, once you have read the book clear through, *you can choose a paragraph anywhere if you are pressed for time and need encouragement or inspiration.*

I have included a list of possible prayer concerns in each of the ten areas of prayer focus. You can check one or more of these items to pray about or you can let them stir your mind to remind you of other personal concerns. Blank spaces are provided below each list of prayer suggestions so you can write in a few words to remind you of any particular prayer needs you don't want to forget. If you fill in those blank spaces with a pencil, as your prayers are answered you can erase what you have written and write in new prayer reminders.

At the end of each area of prayer focus (or chapter), I have provided a sample prayer for you to pray. This prayer can be a beginning point to jumpstart your own prayers as you think of other things to add to it, or it can be the complete prayer in itself.

There are also Scriptures at the end of each prayer that can be read over, proclaimed, spoken aloud, memorized, pondered, meditated on, or simply kept in your heart, however time and inclination lead. Choose one or two or as many as you have time for. I know these Scriptures will be especially encouraging, uplifting, and edifying to you.

If you are pressed for time yet do have a few moments, it is possible to spend 60 seconds on each one of these 10 areas of prayer focus and complete them all in 10 minutes. Trust me, it feels good when you can cover so much ground with the Lord, instead of neglecting certain areas of prayer altogether. But no one is saying you have to limit your praying to 10 minutes. You could spend 10 or 20 minutes on a single area of prayer focus if you want. You could spend an hour on worship alone. No one—especially not God—is holding up a stopwatch and timing you. I am just saying that this *can* be done in 10 minutes, so you will have the peace of knowing you have lifted these important concerns before God's throne. Then you are able to go about the rest of your day and pray for whatever else is pressing on your heart when you have found the right time to do so.

For your convenience, near the end of the book is a condensed version of these ten areas of prayer focus, so that once you have read the book and filled in the blanks with your own personal concerns, you can just flip to this section at the end if you are especially pressed for time, and go through it in however many minutes you have.

At the very end of the book are blank pages under the title of "Answers to Prayer" for you to write in. I pray that you will soon have those pages filled to overflowing. Shall we begin?

WORSHIP AND PRAISE GOD FOR WHO HE IS

Worshipping God is one of the most powerful things we can do. Praising Him takes the focus off of ourselves and puts it entirely on Him. And that is always the best way to approach God and begin to pray.

Prayer is communicating with God. And communicating your love, gratitude, worship, and praise to God is the best way to start any prayer. It is also healthy for your mind and soul, as well as your physical body. Too often in our busy day we don't worship and praise God to the extent we should. He desires more praise than we give Him because He has so much more He wants to give *us*. When we praise Him, He reveals Himself to us. And He wants to reveal as much of Himself to us as we can

receive. Great things happen when we worship God—
far more than we even realize.

Worship Is...

opening your heart to God

inviting the presence of God to dwell with you

praising God as your Creator

exalting Him as the God of love

honoring and thanking God for all He has
done

thanking Jesus for all He accomplished on the
cross

coming in contact with all that God is

allowing God's holiness to touch you

offering yourself to the Lord

demonstrating your love for God

affirming your loyalty to the Lord

lifting your heart and mind to God

preparing to receive all God has for you

acknowledging God as almighty and all-
powerful

letting go of all else and embracing only the
Lord

No matter what is happening in your life, God is always
worthy of your praise. That's why worship must be your

first reaction to everything. It should become a way of life—a priority. You can decide to wake up in the morning thankful to God, because you know He loves you more than you can ever fully understand. Start your day by praising and worshipping Him for all that He is. And remember some of the many ways that worshipping God affects your life.

Ten of the Countless Ways Worshipping God Affects Me

Worship requires an act of my will.

Worship is a choice I make every day.

Worship softens my heart and builds my faith.

Worship enables me to become more like the Lord.

Worship is a powerful weapon of my spiritual warfare.

Worship helps me to hear God speaking to my heart.

Worship evaporates all my fears.

Worship invites God to pour Himself into me.

Worship deepens my relationship with the Lord.

Worship changes my mind, heart, and attitude.

There are countless reasons why you should praise God. Even remembering just one of them will be motivation enough for you to worship and praise Him many times throughout your day—especially each time you pray.

Ten Good Reasons Why I Give Praise to God

I praise God because He is worthy of my praise.

"Give to the LORD the glory due His name; bring an offering, and come into His courts. Oh, worship the LORD in the beauty of holiness! Tremble before Him, all the earth" (Psalm 96:8-9).

I praise God because it brings me into His Presence.

"Oh come, let us sing to the LORD! Let us shout joyfully to the Rock of our salvation. Let us come before His presence with thanksgiving; let us shout joyfully to Him with psalms. For the LORD is the great God, and the great King above all gods" (Psalm 95:1-3).

I praise God because He hears my prayers.

"Now we know that God does not hear sinners; but if anyone is a worshiper of God and does His will, He hears him" (John 9:31).

I praise God because it brings pleasure to my soul.

"Praise the LORD! For it is good to sing praises to our God; for it is pleasant, and praise is beautiful" (Psalm 147:1).

I praise God because He does so much for me.

"He heals the brokenhearted and binds up their wounds. He counts the number of the stars; He calls them all by name. Great is our Lord, and mighty in power; His understanding is infinite. The LORD lifts up the humble; He casts the wicked down to the ground. Sing to the LORD with thanksgiving; sing praises on the harp to our God" (Psalm 147:3-7).

I praise God because He guides me in all things.

"I will bless the LORD who has given me counsel; my heart also instructs me in the night seasons. I have set the LORD always before me; because He is at my right hand I shall not be moved. Therefore my heart is glad, and my glory rejoices; my flesh also will rest in hope" (Psalm 16:7-9).

I praise God because He delivers me and sets me free.

"Offer to God thanksgiving, and pay your vows to the Most High. Call upon Me in the day of trouble; I will deliver you, and you shall glorify Me" (Psalm 50:14-15).

I praise God because He saves me in every way possible.

"Whoever offers praise glorifies Me; and to him who orders his conduct aright I will show the salvation of God" (Psalm 50:23).

I praise God because He protects me in times of trouble.

"He who dwells in the secret place of the Most High shall abide under the shadow of the Almighty. I will say of the LORD, 'He is my refuge and my fortress; my God, in Him I will trust.' Surely He shall deliver you from the snare of the fowler and from the perilous pestilence...

He shall call upon Me, and I will answer him; I will be with him in trouble; I will deliver him and honor him. With long life I will satisfy him, and show him My salvation" (Psalm 91:1-3, 15-16).

I praise God because He heals me and gives me life.

"I will extol You, O LORD, for You have lifted me up, and have not let my foes rejoice over me. O LORD my God, I cried out to You, and You healed me. O LORD, You brought my soul up from the grave; You have kept me alive, that I should not go down to the pit. Sing praise to the LORD, you saints of His, and give thanks at the remembrance of His holy name" (Psalm 30:1-4).

Calling on God by Name

In the Bible, God is referred to by many names. And there are also many words that describe His attributes. I believe the reason for this is that we cannot begin to understand all of who God is without these names and descriptions. The Bible was written to help us know God and understand His ways. The more we know about God, the more we will be able to praise, worship, appreciate, and thank Him in the passionate way He should be acknowledged.

Each of the names of the Lord shows us an aspect of His nature and His attributes. When we acknowledge and praise Him for who He is, our faith in His ability and desire to be that to us increases. The Bible says, "The name of the LORD is a strong tower; the righteous run to it and are safe" (Proverbs 18:10). "Our help is in the name of the LORD, who made heaven and earth" (Psalm 124:8).

The first name you should thank God for being to you is your *heavenly Father*. When the disciples asked Jesus to teach them how to pray, Jesus gave them the Lord's Prayer, which begins by acknowledging God as our Father in heaven. When you begin your prayer that way, it helps you to remember that you are truly one of His children. And this is an extremely important aspect of your relationship with God.

The second most important name to remember is *Jesus*. Never underestimate the power resident in His name. Jesus said, "If you ask anything in My name, I will do it" (John 14:14). If you want to see answers to your prayers, ask in Jesus' name—which is the name above all names.

Below are some of the names and attributes of God that are found in the Bible. Read them all and then choose at least one or more of them each time you pray, and thank Him for being that to you.

Names and Attributes of God

"Lord, I praise You and thank You for being my…"

Mighty God and Everlasting Father

"Unto us a Child is born, unto us a Son is given; and the government will be upon His shoulder. And His name will be called Wonderful, Counselor, Mighty God, Everlasting Father, Prince of Peace" (Isaiah 9:6).

Healer

To you who fear My name the Sun of Righteousness shall arise with healing in His wings" (Malachi 4:2).

Peace

"He Himself is our peace, who has made both one, and has broken down the middle wall of separation" (Ephesians 2:14).

Deliverer

"I am poor and needy; make haste to me, O God! You are my help and my deliverer; O LORD, do not delay" (Psalm 70:5).

Counselor

"I will bless the LORD who has given me counsel; my heart also instructs me in the night seasons" (Psalm 16:7).

Restorer

"He restores my soul; He leads me in the paths of righteousness for His name's sake" (Psalm 23:3).

Redeemer

"'The Redeemer will come to Zion, and to those who turn from transgression in Jacob,' says the Lord" (Isaiah 59:20).

Power of God

"To those who are called, both Jews and Greeks, Christ [is] the power of God and the wisdom of God" (1 Corinthians 1:24).

Resting Place

"My people have been lost sheep. Their shepherds have led them astray; they have turned them away on the mountains. They have gone from mountain to hill; they have forgotten their resting place" (Jeremiah 50:6).

A Strength to the Poor and a Refuge from the Storm

"You have been a strength to the poor, a strength to the needy in his distress, a refuge from the storm, a shade from the heat; for the blast of the terrible ones is as a storm against the wall" (Isaiah 25:4).

God of Gods who is Mighty and Awesome

"The Lord your God is God of gods and Lord of lords, the great God, mighty and awesome, who shows no partiality nor takes a bribe" (Deuteronomy 10:17).

King of Kings and Lord of Lords

"These will make war with the Lamb, and the Lamb will overcome them, for He is Lord of lords and King of kings; and those who are with Him are called, chosen, and faithful" (Revelation 17:14).

Stronghold in the Day of Trouble

"The LORD is good, a stronghold in the day of trouble; and He knows those who trust in Him" (Nahum 1:7).

Shield

"Our soul waits for the LORD; He is our help and our shield" (Psalm 33:20).

Hiding Place

"You are my hiding place; You shall preserve me from trouble; You shall surround me with songs of deliverance" (Psalm 32:7).

Hope

"You are my hope, O Lord GOD; You are my trust from my youth" (Psalm 71:5).

Savior

"My spirit has rejoiced in God my Savior" (Luke 1:47).

Strength and Song

"Behold, God is my salvation, I will trust and not be afraid; 'for YAH, the LORD, is my strength and song; He also has become my salvation'" (Isaiah 12:2).

Helper

"I will pray the Father, and He will give you another Helper, that He may abide with you forever" (John 14:16).

Lifter of My Head

"You, O LORD, are a shield for me, my glory and the One who lifts up my head" (Psalm 3:3).

Holy Spirit and Teacher

"The Holy Spirit will teach you in that very hour what you ought to say" (Luke 12:12).

Comforter and Giver of Mercy

"Sing, O heavens! Be joyful, O earth! And break out in singing, O mountains! For the Lord has comforted His people, and will have mercy on His afflicted" (Isaiah 49:13).

Provider

"My God shall supply all your need according to His riches in glory by Christ Jesus" (Philippians 4:19).

You will find that there is a name for God that answers to every need you have. Write down a list of things you need in your life on the lines provided. Then next to each one write a name of God that answers to that need. You can choose from the list above or choose another name or attribute of God that you have found elsewhere in the Bible.

What I Need	God's Name that Answers to My Need

Prayer Power

Lord, I come before Your presence with thanksgiving. I worship You this day as the almighty Creator of heaven and earth. You are the all-powerful God of the universe for whom nothing is impossible. I exalt You as my Creator, and I praise You as my heavenly Father. I thank You that You are the God of love, peace, and joy. "I will praise You, O LORD, with my whole heart; I will tell of all Your marvelous works. I will be glad and rejoice in You; I will sing praise to Your name, O Most High" (Psalm 9:1-2). I thank You for all that You are.

Thank You for sending Your Son Jesus to be my Savior and Redeemer. Thank You, Jesus, for the price You paid to save me. Thank You for rescuing me, forgiving me, and giving me new life. Thank You for the gift of Your

Holy Spirit in me. Thank You, Holy Spirit, for guiding me, comforting me, and filling me afresh with love, peace, and power. Thank You for Your Word that gives me life. I praise You, Lord, for Your goodness, grace, and mercy that endure forever.

In Jesus' name I pray.

WORD POWER

*By Him let us continually offer the sacrifice
of praise to God, that is, the fruit of our
lips, giving thanks to His name.*

HEBREWS 13:15

*The hour is coming, and now is, when the true
worshipers will worship the Father in spirit and
truth; for the Father is seeking such to worship Him.*

JOHN 4:23

*Vows made to You are binding upon me, O
God; I will render praises to You, for You have
delivered my soul from death. Have You not
kept my feet from falling, that I may walk
before God in the light of the living?*

PSALM 56:12-13

Whoever confesses Me before men, him I will also
confess before My Father who is in heaven.

MATTHEW 10:32

You are a chosen generation, a royal priesthood, a
holy nation, His own special people, that you
may proclaim the praises of Him who called
you out of darkness into His marvelous light.

1 PETER 2:9

Because he has set his love upon Me, therefore
I will deliver him; I will set him on high,
because he has known My name.

PSALM 91:14

They will call on My name, and I will answer
them. I will say, 'This is My people'; and each
one will say, 'The LORD is my God.'

ZECHARIAH 13:9

DECLARE GOD TO BE LORD OVER YOUR LIFE

The moment we receive Jesus as our Savior, we begin a new life. From that time on, Jesus fully intends to be Lord over *every* area of our life. However, *we* sometimes withhold parts of ourself from Him. We make Jesus Lord over our life initially, but then we deny Him lordship in certain areas for one reason or another—often without even realizing it. We let Him be Lord over our Sundays, but not our Saturday nights. We invite Him to be Lord over our work, but not our finances. We want Him to be Lord over our relationships, but not our personal habits. The best way to make certain that Jesus is Lord over *every* area of our life is to *invite* Him to be. And then *declare* Him to be—frequently and specifically.

We must combat our tendency to want to control things in our life by confessing daily that Jesus is Lord. The Bible says of Jesus, "God also has highly exalted Him and given Him the name which is above every name. That at the name of Jesus every knee should bow, of those in heaven, and of those on earth, and of those under the earth, and that every tongue should confess that Jesus Christ is Lord, to the glory of God the Father" (Philippians 2:9-11). Confessing that Jesus is Lord is a deliberate act of faith, and it helps to remember that *only He* is Lord over every area of our life, and not anyone or anything else. The name of Jesus should cause every area of our heart to bow to Him as Lord.

We use our free will to determine which way we will go—*our* way or *God's* way. Declaring Him to be Lord over our life is submitting our will to God's. It's saying, "Not my will, but Yours be done, Lord." When we proclaim that before the Lord, *our* way will begin to line up with *God's* way.

Say, "Jesus, be Lord over every area of my life," and then name those areas specifically where you feel you struggle with complete surrender to Him. If you are not sure about what those areas are, ask Him. Say, "Lord, is there any part of my heart or life that I have not fully surrendered to You?" If there is, He will show you. But He will not push His way in; He wants to be invited. God wants to share Himself with you, but you must be open to sharing every part of your being with Him.

The Areas of My Life Where I Especially Need Jesus to Be Lord

"Jesus, I pray that You will be Lord over my..."

thoughts	recreation
emotions	body
finances	health
day	health habits
marriage	fears
relationships	time
work	children
future	plans
personal habits	giving
attitude	spending
dreams	decisions
career	words
mind	ministry
Other: _____	_____
_____	_____
_____	_____
_____	_____

Acknowledging Jesus as Lord over your life takes only a few moments each day, but the effects of doing so are enormous and far reaching. When you proclaim Jesus to be Lord over your finances, He will bless them. When you declare Jesus to be Lord over your personal habits, He will help you to better resist bad, unhealthy, destructive, or less-than-beneficial habits. When you invite Him to be Lord over your relationships, you will find good ones growing stronger and bad influences eventually disappearing. All this is simply the effect of having more of Jesus in your life—and who doesn't need that?

Every day declare Jesus to be Lord over every area of your life. Instruct your heart to not bow before anyone or anything else but the Lord of your life.

PRAYER POWER

Jesus, I invite You to be Lord over every area of my life today. I especially pray that You will be Lord over

_____

_____

_____

_____

_____

I submit those areas of my life to You and ask You to reign in them in every way. I want *You* to be in control and not me. Just as Your disciples recognized that You are Lord, so do I acknowledge that You are Lord over all (John 13:13). Help me to love You as my Lord and Savior with all my heart, with all my soul, and with all my mind, just as You commanded in Your Word (Matthew 22:37). Help me to trust in You, Lord, with everything that is in me, and not try to figure out life on my own (Proverbs 3:5).

Jesus, You once questioned why people called You Lord and yet didn't do what You asked them to do (Luke 6:46). Help me to always show evidence of Your lordship in my life by living in obedience to Your ways and laws.

Be Lord over my mind, thoughts, attitude, and emotions. Be Lord over my work, finances, giving, and spending. Be Lord over the way I use my time. Be Lord over all my relationships, my marriage, and my children. Be Lord over my plans, decisions, career, and ministry. Be Lord over my health, habits, and the words I speak. Be Lord over my dreams, fears, and future. I proclaim You Lord over all of my life.

In Jesus' name I pray.

WORD POWER

If we live, we live to the Lord; and if we die, we die to the Lord. Therefore, whether we live or die, we are the Lord's.

ROMANS 14:8

I make known to you that no one speaking by the Spirit of God calls Jesus accursed, and no one can say that Jesus is Lord except by the Holy Spirit.

1 CORINTHIANS 12:3

You call me Teacher and Lord, and you say well, for so I am.

JOHN 13:13

Jesus said to him, "'You shall love the LORD your God with all your heart, with all your soul, and with all your mind.'"

MATTHEW 22:37

The LORD is near to all who call upon Him, to all who call upon Him in truth.

PSALM 145:18

There is born to you this day in the city of
David a Savior, who is Christ the Lord.

LUKE 2:11

Why do you call Me "Lord, Lord," and
do not do the things which I say?

LUKE 6:46

The word which God sent to the children
of Israel, preaching peace through
Jesus Christ—He is Lord of all.

ACTS 10:36

INVITE GOD TO BE IN CHARGE OF YOUR DAY

Have you ever had a day that you were expecting to go a certain way, and then it ended up going in a completely different direction? It didn't turn out the way you expected? You are probably saying to yourself, *Who hasn't?* We've all had days like that; they are part of life. And this can be a good thing or a bad thing. But when we have days like this nearly *every* day, that's a bad thing. We don't need to have our days getting out of control all the time. I have found that when you ask God to be in charge of your day, things go better. Then, even if things *don't* go as you planned and the unexpected happens, you will still have greater peace. You will feel that although it was unexpected to *you*, it wasn't a surprise to *God*.

Every day you face many things, but you can invite God to reign in each one of them. Ask Him to order your steps, clear your path, cover your back, and be in charge of your day. It is especially effective when you do this early on in the day, because you will have greater confidence in knowing that He is in charge of every aspect of it. Jesus taught us to ask for what we need in our day. He said to pray, "Give us this day our daily bread" (Matthew 6:11). This is not a "somewhere-in-the-future" kind of prayer. This is a prayer for our immediate needs.

Even if you do not pray this prayer until the late afternoon, you still have what's left of your day—and night—to submit to Him. But if you are praying this prayer at night, submit the day you just had to Him. Ask Him to be in charge of all that happened and to work redemption where it is needed. Then pray about the next day and all that will be in it.

Whatever you have ahead of you today that concerns you, no matter how little of the day is left, tell God about it. Describe to Him all of the ways you want Him to bless your day and ask Him for guidance and assistance through it. Don't leave out anything. If it is important enough to concern you in any way, then it is important enough to bring before the Lord, for *He* cares about all that *you* care about.

Below is a list of common concerns—some of which you may have today—that you will want to bring before the Lord. Note any you want to remember and add any others you may have in the blank spaces below them.

The Ways in Which I Need the Lord to Guide Me Today

"Lord, today I pray that You will bless my day and be in charge of the…"

> errands I have to do
> bills I need to pay
> work I must accomplish
> conversations I need to have
> decisions I must make
> projects I must start or finish
> concerns I have
> people I need to see
> things I want to accomplish
> ways I need help
> situations I *do not* want to happen
> events I hope *will* happen
> ways I need guidance
> people I must interact with
> e-mail I must send
> letter I must write

phone call I must make
traveling I must do
studying I need to complete
meeting I will attend
skills I need to learn
decisions I have to make
understanding I must have
relationships I want to preserve
purchase I should make
guidance I need

Other:_____

_____

_____

When you pray about your day, don't leave anything to chance. Tell God about specific ways you would like Him to guide you. Say, "Lord, I lift up to You the appointment with my doctor, the meeting with my boss, the phone call with my neighbor, and the thing I must purchase." When you ask God to be in charge of all that, then no matter what happens you know God is in it. Even as you are praying about your day, God will bring to mind things you need to remember that you might not otherwise have thought of if you had not been praying. I have found that when I submit my day to God early in the morning, it is far less likely to get out of control later on.

One of the things you can ask God to help you with each day is being able to speak only words that are pleasing to Him (Psalm 19:14). Unfortunately, it is too easy to speak the wrong words at the wrong time and in an instant do damage to yourself or hurt someone else. This can happen without any intention of doing so. Ask God to help you speak words that bring life to everyone who hears them. Ask Him to fill your heart with His Word and His love. "The preparations of the heart belong to man, but the answer of the tongue is from the LORD" (Proverbs 16:1).

When we prepare our hearts in prayer and in God's Word early in the day, He can guide us in all we say. Jesus said, "Brood of vipers! How can you, being evil, speak good things? For out of the abundance of the heart the mouth speaks" (Matthew 12:34). Ask the Holy Spirit to fill your heart afresh each day with more of Him and His nature so that what comes out of your mouth blesses others and glorifies God.

Invite God to be in charge of your day and ask Him to bring order and success in all that you do. When you do that, you will have a day filled with greater peace and a sense of accomplishment.

PRAYER POWER

Lord, I commit my day to You and ask You to be in charge of it from beginning to end. Enable me to do all I need to do successfully and well. Help me to do it carefully and not carelessly. Help me to do it all diligently and not lazily. Help me to do everything skillfully and not shabbily. I know I cannot do all I need to do in my day without Your help.

I don't want to ever take for granted that, just because I have done some of these things before, they are always going to turn out right each time. I know that sometimes even the simplest things can become a problem or a challenge, so I don't want to assume that everything will automatically go smoothly. That's why I submit my entire day to You and ask You to be in charge of all I am doing.

Specifically, what I need the most help with today is

_____

The ways I want You to guide me today are

_____

What I am most concerned about today is

_____

_____

The things I want to accomplish today are

_____

The people I need to see and talk to are

_____

What I hope will happen today is

_____

What I don't want to happen today is

_____

Lord, I thank You that You are in charge of my day and all that happens. Be in charge of the surprises, the unexpected, and the things that turn out differently than I planned. Enable me to hear Your voice speaking to my heart, telling me the way I should go and what I should do.

In Jesus' name I pray.

WORD POWER

This is the day the LORD has made; we will rejoice and be glad in it.
PSALM 118:24

*In all your ways acknowledge Him, and He
shall direct your paths. Do not be wise in your
own eyes; fear the LORD and depart from evil.*

PROVERBS 3:6-7

*Each one's work will become clear; for the Day will
declare it, because it will be revealed by fire; and
the fire will test each one's work, of what sort it is.*

1 CORINTHIANS 3:13

*Do not boast about tomorrow, for you do
not know what a day may bring forth.*

PROVERBS 27:1

*He who would love life and see good
days, let him refrain his tongue from
evil, and his lips from speaking deceit.*

1 PETER 3:10

*For a day in Your courts is better than a thousand.
I would rather be a doorkeeper in the house of
my God than dwell in the tents of wickedness.*

PSALM 84:10

*Beloved, do not forget this one thing, that
with the Lord one day is as a thousand
years, and a thousand years as one day.*

2 PETER 3:8

SUBMIT YOUR BODY, HEART, AND MIND TO GOD

Your body—including your heart and mind—is the temple of the Holy Spirit. That's why God wants you to take good care of it. Because the Holy Spirit lives in you, caring for your body, mind, and emotions is something you do as much for *Him* as for yourself. While you don't have to be preoccupied with your body, you do have to take care of the temple God has given you. You can't feed it poorly, not give it enough proper exercise, fill it with poison, seldom give it enough rest, and then be critical of it when it doesn't *look* the way you want it to or *do* what you want it to do. You must be grateful for it and treat it well.

God says He wants you to present your body to Him as a living sacrifice. He desires that you be a good steward of the body He has given you. But you need His help in order to do that. Every day you make choices as to what you will do with your body—what you will eat, whether you will exercise, how you will rest, and if you will be obedient to His ways and laws regarding it. Ask God to guide you daily in the care of your health, and seek Him for healing when you need it.

Sometimes we violate God's ways with regard to our body care because we don't know the right things to do. That's why we must ask God to show us what to do and help us to do it. Most of the time, however, we just want to do what we want. We make Jesus Lord over our life, but not over our body or our health care habits. Many of the diseases, injuries, and infirmities we suffer happen because we have violated some of the natural laws of God. We need to ask God to help us live His way with regard to our health habits. When we do, He will guide us (Isaiah 30:21). Our health is too important not to pray about it every day. Below are a number of ways to pray. Choose a few of them each time you pray so that you will become a good steward of your body.

Twenty Ways to Pray About Taking Care of My Body

"Lord, bless my body and help me to…"

eat right and be attracted to health-giving food

get some form of good exercise several times a week

experience sound, rejuvenating sleep

control my stress level

rid myself of all toxins

get proper checkups

not ignore warning signs in my body

take proper supplements as I need them

avoid doing things that will make me sick

take precautions to avoid illness or disease

not overindulge when I eat

avoid foods I know are not good for me

find peace by spending time in prayer and Your Word

simplify my life in every way I can

find peace in simplicity

eat more fruits and vegetables

avoid eating too much sugar

avoid eating too much of anything

avoid ingesting harmful chemicals

eat more natural foods than highly processed foods

When you are mentally and emotionally healthy, you will have peace about who you are and where you are headed in your future. Even if you don't know *exactly* who you are or where you are going, you can still have peace in your mind and emotions about all of that when you know God is in charge. The way to be sure He is in charge of your mind and emotions—your thoughts and feelings—is to ask Him to be.

Twenty Ways to Pray About My Mind and Emotions

"Lord, I pray that You would enable me to…"

> have a clear mind
> have a sound mind
> think positive thoughts
> not allow negativity to rule my attitude
> dwell on the truth
> identify lies
> have peace in my mind and heart
> better handle stress
> have the ability to learn easily
> have a good memory
> not have worry or fear
> refuse to entertain guilt
> be rid of all unforgiveness

have a heart filled with love

resist entertaining bad or upsetting thoughts

be free of all anxiety

live without depression

be rid of all loneliness

be free of perfectionism

experience great joy

Too often we berate ourselves because we do the wrong things with regard to caring for our body, mind, and emotions. We let the guilt we feel—when we do what we know is not right—overcome us and affect our relationship with God. We don't pray as much because we don't feel we deserve to come before God. But God wants us to depend on Him to help us with that too. So instead of feeling badly and criticizing yourself for not being perfect in the area of body care, ask God to enable you to do what you need to do. He will. Ask Him for patience in the process.

PRAYER POWER

Lord, I submit my body to You. Help me to be disciplined in the way I care for it. Help me to choose health-filled and life-giving foods and be able to resist eating what I should not have. Enable me to make the right choices with regard to what I eat. Give me the strength I need to avoid what is not good for me. Help me to always be attracted to food that is beneficial.

Give me the self-discipline I need to properly exercise in order to strengthen my body and rid it of all toxins. Help me to do what is necessary to have good and beneficial rest. Only *You* know what is best for me. Show me things I need to see. Teach me all I must learn. Lead me to the right people to help and advise me. Keep me from doing anything careless or indulgent. Thank You that I am fearfully and wonderfully made (Psalm 139:14). Help me to value and take proper care of the body You have given me.

Thank You, Lord, that You are my Healer. If there is any place in my body right now that is not well or whole, I pray You would heal me completely. Show me whatever I need to see or do. If I should see a doctor, help me to find the right one to go to. The ways I want to be healed today are _____

_____

_____

"Heal me, O LORD, and I shall be healed" (Jeremiah 17:14).

Lord, take control of my mind and emotions. Help me to think clearly. Enable me to discern the truth from a

---

lie and not allow wrong or negative thoughts into my mind. Help me to choose my thoughts carefully and fill my mind with only thoughts and images that are glorifying to You. Thank You that I have the mind of Christ (1 Corinthians 2:16).

Help me to live every day with peace in my heart and mind. Take away all stress and teach me to live a simpler and more contented life. Enable me to see all the good in my life and not dwell on the negatives. Thank You for the sound mind You have given me (2 Timothy 1:7).

The thing I struggle with most in the area of my mind and emotions is _____

_____

_____

The greatest area of stress in my life is _____

_____

_____

Create in me a clean heart that is free of all negativity and unforgiveness. Help me to have Your love and forgiveness in my heart. Enable me to live in peace, tranquility, simplicity, and good health.

In Jesus' name I pray.

WORD POWER

*I will praise You, for I am fearfully and
wonderfully made; marvelous are Your
works, and that my soul knows very well.*

PSALM 139:14

*I beseech you therefore, brethren, by the
mercies of God, that you present your
bodies a living sacrifice, holy, acceptable to
God, which is your reasonable service.*

ROMANS 12:1

The man who fears God will avoid all extremes.

ECCLESIASTES 7:18 NIV

*Heal me, O LORD, and I shall be healed; save
me, and I shall be saved, for You are my praise.*

JEREMIAH 17:14

*"Who has known the mind of the LORD that he may
instruct Him?" But we have the mind of Christ.*

1 CORINTHIANS 2:16

*God has not given us a spirit of fear, but of
power and of love and of a sound mind.*

2 TIMOTHY 1:7

---

*Be anxious for nothing, but in everything by prayer
and supplication, with thanksgiving, let your
requests be made known to God; and the peace
of God, which surpasses all understanding, will
guard your hearts and minds through Christ Jesus.*

PHILIPPIANS 4:6-7

*He will die for lack of discipline, led
astray by his own great folly.*

PROVERBS 5:23 NIV

CONFESS ANY SIN
OF THOUGHT OR ACTION

No one is perfect. None of us does everything right all the time. We all do things we regret. Each one of us has said words that hurt people—even if we had no intention of ever doing that. We all, at one time or another, have had private thoughts that are not right and need to be exposed to the light of the Lord so they can be burned out of us. We all have sinned in some way and have need of the Lord's cleansing.

We don't have to have murdered someone or robbed a bank in order to need to confess our sins. In the Bible, such things as having doubt or jealousy, or being selfish, or gossiping, or telling "white lies," are all clearly revealed to be sin. Confession is the only way to be completely free of the uneasy feelings of guilt we often have but don't fully recognize as such because we don't think we have done anything wrong. When we confess any wrong thought, word, or action, we can be cleansed of all the destructive effects of sin and be completely free of guilt.

One of the main reasons to confess our sins is because sin separates us from God. "Your iniquities have separated you from your God; and your sins have hidden His face from you, so that He will not hear" (Isaiah 59:2). With that Scripture I rest my case for confession. Above all else, we do not want to be separated from God.

The Bible says that if we allow iniquity to stay in our hearts, God won't listen to our prayers (Psalm 66:18). We definitely want God to hear our prayers! We must do whatever He requires so that the lines are kept open between us and Him. We must often ask God to help us recognize anything we have done wrong and admit it. We must also ask Him to enable us to walk away from it and never do it again.

Twenty Good Reasons Why
I Should Confess to God

to be free of all sin
to be completely honest with the Lord
to get right with God
to enjoy all the blessings God has for me

to avoid the consequences of sin

to not allow sin to separate me from God

to know God will hear my prayers

to get free of the heavy burden of sin

to enjoy wholeness of mind and soul

to avoid the death that sin brings

to keep from violating God's laws

to find the only path to true repentance

to receive God's forgiveness

to please God and glorify Him

to have a clear conscience and sleep well at
  night

to avoid destruction in my life

to have nothing holding me back

to move into all God has for me

to be able to flourish and prosper

to enjoy the presence of God

God gives you a way out of all guilt through confession
and repentance. If you feel *convicted* about something
you've done, it will draw you closer to the Lord as you
confess it and ask Him to help you make things right.
However, if you feel *condemned* about something you've
done, you can trust that this comes from the enemy of
your soul, who delights in tormenting you because you
have not confessed or repented of the sin. And sin will

build a wall of separation between you and God, because you feel too guilty to come before Him. The enemy wants you to feel condemned because this will keep you from enjoying a close relationship with the Lord.

If the enemy can get you so full of condemnation that you don't pray because of it, then he has succeeded in his plan. Don't let that happen. Don't let any failure or mistake you make separate you from God. Confess and repent of it immediately. Refuse to allow it to grow into something the enemy can use against you.

The last thing you need to carry around in your life is guilt. If you have disobeyed God's laws in any way, confess that to Him and receive His forgiveness and cleansing. If you are feeling bad about something, bring it to Him in prayer. If you feel guilty because you have not chosen God's best for your life, ask Him to help you make better choices. If you can't think of anything to confess, ask God to show you whatever you might not be seeing. Below is a list that can help you examine your heart and actions.

Some Things I May Need to Confess

thoughts that are not glorifying to God
wrong words I have spoken
doubt I have had
secret attitudes that do not please the Lord

dishonesty

lack of integrity

lies I have led others to believe

critical thoughts or words

rudeness

lovelessness

taking something that is not mine

jealousy

prideful attitude

arrogance

fear due to doubting God

insensitivity to the needs of others

lack of generosity

impatience

discontentment with my life

lack of faith in the Lord

Ask God every day to show you the truth about yourself. It's easy to overlook certain things. He will bring to mind what you need to see, and when He does, confess what He reveals to you. Even something that seems little to you can be big enough to affect your intimacy with the Lord. Don't let that happen to you. Make confession a part of your prayers every day. It may well be that you have nothing to confess, but at least you have inquired of the Lord about it. And that will give you confidence and assurance before Him.

Prayer Power

Lord, help me to be free of all sin and its consequences. Reveal to me anything in my heart and mind that should not be there. Show me any place where I am missing the mark You have for me. Help me to see the truth about myself. Reveal to me where I am doing things wrong and help me to see that clearly so I can confess it to You. Enable me to make corrections where they need to be made. You, Lord, know the secrets of my heart (Psalm 44:21). Reveal to me anything that is in my heart today that is not right. Cleanse me of my secret faults (Psalm 19:12).

Lord, I know that if I confess my sins, You are faithful and just to forgive me of my sins and to cleanse me from all unrighteousness (1 John 1:9). Specifically, I confess to You _____

I repent of this and ask You to forgive me. Help me to not do this anymore. Help me to stay free of the death that is the consequence of sin (Romans 6:23). I know that sin is a burden that is too heavy for me to carry (Psalm 38:3-5).

Lord, I know that if my heart does not condemn me, I can have confidence in Your presence, and whatever I ask of You I will receive because I am doing what is pleasing to You (1 John 3:21-22). More than anything I want to have a heart that is completely free of guilt and condemnation.

Cleanse me and set me free of all sin so that I can please You and You will answer my prayers.

In Jesus' name I pray.

WORD POWER

He who covers his sins will not prosper, but whoever confesses and forsakes them will have mercy.

PROVERBS 28:13

Repent therefore and be converted, that your sins may be blotted out, so that times of refreshing may come from the presence of the Lord.

ACTS 3:19

Blessed is he whose transgression is forgiven, whose sin is covered.

PSALM 32:1

Create in me a clean heart, O God, and renew a steadfast spirit within me. Do not cast me away from Your presence, and do not take Your Holy Spirit from me. Restore to me the joy of Your salvation, and uphold me by Your generous Spirit.

PSALM 51:10-12

If I regard iniquity in my heart, the Lord will not hear.

PSALM 66:18

*If we say that we have no sin, we deceive ourselves,
and the truth is not in us. If we confess our
sins, He is faithful and just to forgive us our sins
and to cleanse us from all unrighteousness.*

1 JOHN 1:8-9

*Beloved, if our heart does not condemn us, we
have confidence toward God. And whatever
we ask we receive from Him, because we
keep His commandments and do those
things that are pleasing in His sight.*

1 JOHN 3:21-22

*Search me, O God, and know my heart; try me, and
know my anxieties; and see if there is any wicked
way in me, and lead me in the way everlasting.*

PSALM 139:23-24

SEEK GOD'S PROTECTION AND COVERING

God promises in His Word that He will protect us. But because the promises of God are appropriated in prayer, this is something that we need to pray about every day. God promises, for example, that no weapon formed against us will prosper (Isaiah 54:17). But we still have to appropriate that promise with our prayers. We can say, "Lord, I thank You for Your Word that promises to Your servants that no weapon formed against us will prosper. Therefore, I pray that no plan of the enemy against me will succeed."

There may be times when you must call on the Lord for help in a sudden emergency. Freak accidents, serious illness, financial problems, crime, and natural disasters can all strike without warning. Sometimes God protects us *from* it, and sometimes He protects us *in* it and *through* it. But you will have greater confidence in the midst of something like that if you know you have been praying for God's protection all along. That's why it is better to pray for His protection in advance of anything bad happening instead of waiting until disaster strikes.

Eighteen Ways I Need God's Protection

"Lord, the areas where I most need Your protection today are for my..."

> physical body (protection from diseases or injuries)
> travels (from accidents in a plane or car)
> home (from fire or break-in)
> car (from theft or breakdown)
> property (from damage or loss)
> business (from failure or bad decisions)
> reputation (from slander or scandal)
> family (from accidents or illness)
> finances (from poor judgment or bad investments)
> marriage (from strife or miscommunication)
> friendships (from offense or misunderstanding)
> mind (from confusion or lack of clarity)

emotions (from depression or anxiety)

relationships (from trouble or friction)

work (from disability or disfavor)

environment (from natural disasters or dangers)

neighborhood (from thieves or murderers)

health (from food poisoning or contagious diseases)

Other: _____

_____

_____

God knows that there are far too many things in our world to be worried about, but He also knows we spend far too much time worrying about these things. He wants us, instead, to cast our cares on Him as we pray specifically regarding everything that concerns us about our safety. You will live with greater peace in your mind and soul if you come before the Lord each day and tell Him about the things that concern you.

Eight Things I Can Do in Response to God's Promises of Protection

I can call on the Lord.

"I will call upon the Lord, who is worthy to be praised; so shall I be saved from my enemies" (Psalm 18:3).

I can trust in God's Word and His promises for my safety.

"I will both lie down in peace, and sleep; for You alone, O Lord, make me dwell in safety" (Psalm 4:8).

I can hide myself in the Lord.

"Keep me as the apple of Your eye; hide me under the shadow of Your wings, from the wicked who oppress me, from my deadly enemies who surround me" (Psalm 17:8-9).

I can obey God.

"Know that the Lord has set apart for Himself him who is godly; the Lord will hear when I call to Him. Be angry, and do not sin. Meditate within your heart on your bed, and be still" (Psalm 4:3-4).

I can pray for protection.

"Hear me when I call, O God of my righteousness! You have relieved me in my distress; have mercy on me, and hear my prayer" (Psalm 4:1).

I can live in the fear of the Lord.

"In the fear of the Lord there is strong confidence, and His children will have a place of refuge. The fear of the Lord is a fountain of life, to turn one away from the snares of death" (Proverbs 14:26-27).

I can praise God.

"Vows made to You are binding upon me, O God; I will render praises to You, for You have delivered my soul from death. Have You not kept my feet from falling, that I may walk before God in the light of the living?" (Psalm 56:12-13)

I can put my trust in the Lord.

"Let all those rejoice who put their trust in You; let them ever shout for joy, because You defend them; let those also who love Your name be joyful in You. For You, O Lord, will bless the righteous; with favor You will surround him as with a shield" (Psalm 5:11-12).

Don't take God for granted by neglecting to pray for the protection He has for you. Ask God to help you call upon His name, trust in Him, hide yourself in Him, live in obedience to His ways, believe the promises in His Word for your protection, and have the fear of the Lord in your heart.

PRAYER POWER

Lord, I pray that You would protect me from all dangers, accidents, diseases, and evil influences. Hide me in Your shadow and keep me safe from the wicked wherever I go (Psalm 17:8). Protect my dwelling place from any intruders or disasters. Protect me from anyone with evil intent, and from all plans of the enemy.

Protect me in cars, on planes, wherever I walk, or whatever I do. Give me the wisdom to always be in the right place at the right time. Enable me to discern Your will so that I will continuously move in the center of it. Send your angels to surround me and keep me so safe that I don't ever stumble. Thank You that You are "a very present help in trouble" (Psalm 46:1). Thank You that no weapon formed against me will prosper (Isaiah 54:17). Protect me from all dangers and disasters.

I praise You for being my Protector every day. Thank You for all the times You have protected me from death and disaster in the past—and especially those times when I wasn't even aware of it. Thank You for surrounding me like a shield (Psalm 5:11-12). Thank You for setting me in the safety for which I yearn (Psalm 12:5). Thank You that I don't have to be afraid of the dangers that are all around me, night and day (Psalm 91:5-7). Thank You that You have given Your angels charge over me to protect me (Psalm 91:11-12). You are my refuge in the day of trouble (Psalm 59:16-17).

In Jesus' name I pray.

WORD POWER

"No weapon formed against you shall prosper,
and every tongue which rises against you in
judgment you shall condemn. This is the

heritage of the servants of the LORD, and their
righteousness is from Me," says the LORD.

ISAIAH 54:17

When you pass through the waters, I will be with
you; and through the rivers, they shall not overflow
you. When you walk through the fire, you shall
not be burned, nor shall the flame scorch you.

ISAIAH 43:2

He shall cover you with His feathers, and under
His wings you shall take refuge; His truth shall be
your shield and buckler. You shall not be afraid of
the terror by night, nor of the arrow that flies by
day, nor of the pestilence that walks in darkness, nor
of the destruction that lays waste at noonday. A
thousand may fall at your side, and ten thousand
at your right hand; but it shall not come near you.

PSALM 91:4-7

Because you have made the LORD, who is my refuge,
even the Most High, your dwelling place, no evil
shall befall you, nor shall any plague come near your
dwelling; for He shall give His angels charge over you,
to keep you in all your ways. In their hands they shall
bear you up, lest you dash your foot against a stone.

PSALM 91:9-12

---

*I will sing of Your power; yes, I will sing aloud
of Your mercy in the morning; for You have
been my defense and refuge in the day of my
trouble. To You, O my Strength, I will sing
praises; for God is my defense, my God of mercy.*

PSALM 59:16-17

*I will both lie down in peace, and sleep; for You
alone, O LORD, make me dwell in safety.*

PSALM 4:8

*"For the oppression of the poor, for the sighing of
the needy, now I will arise," says the LORD; "I
will set him in the safety for which he yearns."*

PSALM 12:5

TELL GOD THE DESIRES
OF YOUR HEART

God cares about you. And He cares about what you care about. The Bible says that God opens His hand and satisfies the desire of every living thing (Psalm 145:16). But it doesn't automatically happen—as you probably well know. Something is required of you. God wants you to pray. God knows what you need, but you still have to ask Him for it. Just as salvation is free, yet we don't get saved without praying, so God's provision is His gift to us, but He still wants us to ask Him for it in faith that He will provide.

God wants you to pray about all that concerns you—no matter how big or how small it seems to you. He wants you to tell Him everything that is in your heart. And He wants you to persist in prayer without giving up. It is written of Jesus that "He spoke a parable to them, that men always ought to pray and not lose heart" (Luke 18:1). Too often if we don't get the answer we want right away, we become impatient and discouraged. We stop praying because we think that if God didn't answer in the time and way we wanted Him to, then He is not going to answer at all. But God wants us to "continue earnestly in prayer, being vigilant in it with thanksgiving" (Colossians 4:2).

God wants us to ask Him for even our most basic needs. Jesus taught us to pray, "Give us this day our daily bread" (Matthew 6:11). There is surely no need in our lives more immediate or basic than knowing where our next meal is coming from. And God already knows we need to eat; after all He created us that way. Yet He wants us to *ask* Him to *provide* it for us. That's the way He works. We *ask; He provides.* He is not requiring us to do that in order to force us to grovel, but because He wants us to depend on Him for everything. Our asking declares our dependence upon Him. It also declares our faith in His ability and desire to provide for us.

God wants you to seek Him for all your needs so you can receive all He has for you. He desires that you knock on the door of heaven so He can open it for you (Matthew 7:7-8). He wants you to ask of Him without giving up.

That means you must keep asking, seeking, and knocking every day.

We usually don't have to be reminded of the things we need, because they are always in the forefront of our mind. But often we *do* need to be reminded to *pray* about them. Too often we *worry* about things instead of *asking God* for them. Check out this brief list below for some of the daily needs you may have forgotten to pray about on an ongoing basis.

Important Things I Need from God Today

"Lord, today I need..."

> finances to pay all of my bills
> favor with the people I will see
> good communication with my spouse
> peace reigning between my family members
> the ability to care for my children
> the strength to do all I must do
> provision and protection for my home
> help to make all the right decisions
> the capability to do well in my work
> success in all my business ventures
> the knowledge of when to say yes or no

---

doors of opportunity for advancement to open

wisdom about making a purchase or an
   investment

guidance for how to use my time wisely

understanding of certain things

help being organized and productive

the capacity to get things done

Other: _____

_____

_____

You don't have to pray for every single one of these things every day, but you should mention each of them from time to time. Anything that causes you concern should be prayed about. And anything that you *don't want* to cause you concern in the future should be prayed about as well. God says to not be anxious about anything but to pray about everything so that you will have unfathomable peace (Philippians 4:6-7). He wants to do so much more in your life than you can even think of to ask for, and He will do it by the power of the Holy Spirit who lives in you. "To Him who is able to do exceedingly abundantly above all that we ask or think, according to the power that works in us, to Him be glory in the church by Christ Jesus to all generations, forever and ever. Amen" (Ephesians 3:20-21).

Tell God everything you need today and all that your heart desires. Bring every one of your needs, concerns, fears, and hopes to Him. "Whatever things you ask in prayer, believing, you will receive" (Matthew 21:22). Remember that nothing is too large or too small for God to handle.

PRAYER POWER

Lord, I thank You that You will provide for all my needs and You want to give me the desires of my heart when I delight myself in You (Psalm 37:4). Your Word says that You will "perfect that which concerns me" (Psalm 138:8). I thank You in advance for Your perfecting work in my life and in these concerns I pray about today. I put them all in Your hands, and I release the burden of them to You. I pray that You would meet all of my needs today.

I pray that my family and I will always have a secure home to live in and good food to eat. Specifically I lift before You my greatest needs today, which are _____

_____

_____

The greatest desires of my heart today are _____

_____

_____

Thank You for always providing for my needs in the past. Thank You that You will continue to provide for me in the future, just as You have promised in Your Word. Show me how I can be of service to You by helping to meet the needs of others.

In Jesus' name I pray.

WORD POWER

Delight yourself also in the LORD, and He shall give you the desires of your heart.
PSALM 37:4

Be anxious for nothing, but in everything by prayer and supplication, with thanksgiving, let your requests be made known to God; and the peace of God, which surpasses all understanding, will guard your hearts and minds through Christ Jesus.
PHILIPPIANS 4:6-7

Seek the kingdom of God, and all these things shall be added to you.
LUKE 12:31

*If you then, being evil, know how to give good gifts
to your children, how much more will your heavenly
Father give the Holy Spirit to those who ask Him!*

Luke 11:13

*Ask, and it will be given to you; seek, and you will
find; knock, and it will be opened to you. For
everyone who asks receives, and he who seeks
finds, and to him who knocks it will be opened.*

Matthew 7:7-8

*Do not fear, little flock, for it is your Father's
good pleasure to give you the kingdom.*

Luke 12:32

*If you abide in Me, and My words abide in you, you
will ask what you desire, and it shall be done for you.*

John 15:7

*Whatever you ask in My name, that I will do,
that the Father may be glorified in the Son. If
you ask anything in My name, I will do it.*

John 14:13-14

PRAY FOR THE PEOPLE IN YOUR LIFE

In each of our lives there are so many people who need prayer that it is hard to remember to pray for them all each day. I find that the best way to do this is to start praying for the people closest to you—your immediate family and friends. Then move beyond them to your extended family and acquaintances. Pray for the people you will see in your day or week—the people at work, at church, and at the stores or offices where you go. Ask God to bring to mind anyone who especially needs your prayers, and He will remind you of someone you might not have otherwise thought of to pray for.

Below is a list of people that will help you remember those you may want to pray for today. Don't let this list become intimidating because it is not necessary to pray for every person each day. Ask the Holy Spirit to guide you as you choose which ones to pray for and when. This list will help you to think of those who might need prayer more than others, and it will enable you to remember someone you might otherwise have forgotten. There is space below for you to write in any other people you especially want to bring before the throne of God.

People in My Life Who Need Prayer

"Lord, today I pray for…"

> my husband/my wife
> my mother/my father
> my brother/my sister
> my son/my daughter
> my grandchildren
> my stepchildren
> my son-in-law/my daughter-in-law
> my mother-in-law/my father-in-law
> my aunt/my uncle
> my cousins
> my roommate
> my close friends
> my acquaintances/my casual friends
> my extended family members

my neighbors

my pastor and church leaders

the people I work with

the people I see in my day

the people at the appointments I keep

the people at my church

the people who are difficult to deal with

the person I dread seeing

the person I find hard to talk to

the people I am aware of who need help

the people I know of who need healing

the people I've heard about on the news

the person who is most on my heart today

Other: _____

_____

_____

_____

Once you have prayed about a person, release him or her into God's hands. That doesn't mean you don't pray about him or her again when you think of that person, but give yourself some moments of relief from that burden on your heart. Enjoy the peace of knowing you have surrendered that person and situation to God and He has heard your prayers and will answer in His way and His time.

If you ever find yourself becoming impatient when you don't see your prayers for other people answered as fast as you would like, keep in mind that you are interceding for someone who has a will and a destiny separate from yours. Remember that you are *partnering* with God to see *His* will done. It's *your* job to *pray,* and it's God's job to *answer.* You just need to do *your* job and let God do *His.* Trust Him to answer your prayers for others in the time and way He decides.

Good relationships are important to each of us. They build us up and edify us. They keep us balanced and accountable. It is not healthy to be isolated. You need people in your life who will stand *with* you and *by* you. You need solid relationships where the good in *them* rubs off on *you,* and the good in *you* affects *them* in that same way.

Five Reasons Why I Need Good, Godly Friends

I need to know that someone loves me.

"A friend loves at all times, and a brother is born for adversity" (Proverbs 17:17).

I need to learn how to be a good friend to others.

"A man who has friends must himself be friendly, but there is a friend who sticks closer than a brother" (Proverbs 18:24).

I need someone I can go to for advice.

"Ointment and perfume delight the heart, and the sweetness of a man's friend gives delight by hearty counsel" (Proverbs 27:9).

I need someone who can help in times of trouble.

"Two are better than one, because they have a good reward for their labor. For if they fall, one will lift up his companion. But woe to him who is alone when he falls, for he has no one to help him up" (Ecclesiastes 4:9-10).

I need people with whom we can be good for one another.

"As iron sharpens iron, so a man sharpens the countenance of his friend" (Proverbs 27:17).

In order to have good friends and relationships, we have to *be* a good friend *in* a relationship. There are certain ways God wants us to conduct ourselves with people that always reap great rewards. When we relate to others the way the Bible instructs us to, we are investing in these valuable relationships.

Seven Ways I Should Relate to the People in My Life

Lord, help me to relate to others with love.

"Since you have purified your souls in obeying the truth through the Spirit in sincere love of the brethren, love one another fervently with a pure heart" (1 Peter 1:22).

Lord, help me to relate to others with affection.

"Be kindly affectionate to one another with brotherly love, in honor giving preference to one another" (Romans 12:10).

Lord, help me to relate to others with compassion.

"Finally, all of you be of one mind, having compassion for one another; love as brothers, be tenderhearted, be courteous" (1 Peter 3:8).

Lord, help me to relate to others with care.

"There should be no schism in the body, but that the members should have the same care for one another" (1 Corinthians 12:25).

Lord, help me to relate to others with a servant's heart.

"You, brethren, have been called to liberty; only do not use liberty as an opportunity for the flesh, but through love serve one another" (Galatians 5:13).

Lord, help me to relate to others with forgiveness and kindness.

"Let all bitterness, wrath, anger, clamor, and evil speaking be put away from you, with all malice. And be kind to one another, tenderhearted, forgiving one another, just as God in Christ forgave you" (Ephesians 4:31-32).

Lord, help me to relate to others with peace.

"Salt is good, but if the salt loses its flavor, how will you season it? Have salt in yourselves, and have peace with one another" (Mark 9:50).

Good relationships are crucial to your well-being, but they can be too easily destroyed or damaged. I have found that it is much easier to *protect* them in prayer than to try to repair them after the damage has already been done. However, God can restore a relationship that has been strained, injured, or broken when you pray about it. If there is a problem in any relationship you have, or there is one that gives you great concern, ask God to help you reconcile your differences and bring healing.

Don't leave any of your relationships to chance. Pray about each one. Bring them before the throne of God. And pray for those who are difficult to love as well. Remember, you always grow to love the people you pray for. As you pray, God gives you *His* heart of love for them.

PRAYER POWER

Lord, help me to always have compassion and love in my heart for others. Help me to treat everyone with affection, kindness, and care. Give me a servant's heart. Help me to forgive easily and quickly. Enable me to be a peacemaker in every relationship that I have—especially with the people I live with or am closest to.

Lord, I lift up to You my family members. Specifically, I pray for _____

_____

I lift up to You my friends and acquaintances. I especially want to pray for _____

_____

_____

.

I also lift up to You the people at my work: _____

_____

_____

I lift up to You the people I will see in my day: _____

_____

_____

The person most on my heart today is: _____

_____

_____

For that person I want to pray _____

_____

_____

I lift all of these people to You and ask You to bless them today with Your love, peace, health, prosperity, and success. Pour out Your Spirit upon them and help them to know You better.

Lord, show me if I have any feelings toward anyone that are less than forgiving. Specifically I pray about _____

_____

_____

I confess any unforgiveness I have in me as sin. Deliver me and keep me free of all unforgiveness.

Lord, I ask that Your peace would reign in my most difficult or troubling relationships. Help us to come to a place of peace and unity. Where there has been a misunderstanding, I pray that You would bring clarity and reconciliation. Help me to be Your light to anyone who doesn't know You. Specifically, I pray for _____

_____

_____

Open this person's heart to receive You.

Help me to choose my friends wisely. Give me discernment so that I can separate myself from someone who is dangerous or will be a bad influence. Bless every relationship I have. Help me to be a good influence on all who know me. Teach me to be a good friend to others. Help me to never leave my relationships to chance, but to pray about them instead.

In Jesus' name I pray.

WORD POWER

The righteous should choose his friends carefully,
for the way of the wicked leads them astray.
PROVERBS 12:26

Bear one another's burdens, and
so fulfill the law of Christ.
GALATIANS 6:2

Moreover, as for me, far be it from me that I should
sin against the LORD in ceasing to pray for you;
but I will teach you the good and the right way.
1 SAMUEL 12:23

Confess your trespasses to one another, and pray for
one another, that you may be healed. The effective,
fervent prayer of a righteous man avails much.
JAMES 5:16

Do not enter the path of the wicked, and
do not walk in the way of evil.
PROVERBS 4:14

Do not be unequally yoked together with unbelievers.
For what fellowship has righteousness with

lawlessness? And what communion has light with darkness? And what accord has Christ with Belial? Or what part has a believer with an unbeliever?

2 Corinthians 6:14-15

If there is any consolation in Christ, if any comfort of love, if any fellowship of the Spirit, if any affection and mercy, fulfill my joy by being like-minded, having the same love, being of one accord, of one mind. Let nothing be done through selfish ambition or conceit, but in lowliness of mind let each esteem others better than himself. Let each of you look out not only for his own interests, but also for the interests of others.

Philippians 2:1-4

INTERCEDE FOR THE WORLD AROUND YOU

God asks each one of us to intercede for our community, nation, and the world, and He wants us to pray for our leaders as well (1 Timothy 2:1-4). However, we often don't pray about these things because they seem too big and far removed from us and our daily lives. We tend to think, *How much difference could my little prayer make with these enormous issues?* But praying for our nation, our leaders, and the world around us is not an option; it is a mandate from God. It's something we all are required to do.

God wants you to be His intercessor. An intercessor is someone who stands before God and prays for another. In the Bible, God looked for someone to stand in the gap before Him and pray for the land so it wouldn't be destroyed because of all the evil in it. But the sad part was He "found no one" (Ezekiel 22:30). God had to bring judgment on the land because He could not find one person to intercede on behalf of the people. You and I can answer God's call every day to intercede for people and situations that need the touch of His hand and the effect of His power on their behalf. Every day you can partner with God to see His purposes fulfilled on earth. Below are some of the ways you can pray, but don't be overwhelmed by this list. Just choose one or two of them each time you pray.

Thirty Ways to Intercede for the World Around Me

"Lord, I pray for the world around me that You will..."

> protect my neighbors
> keep my neighborhood safe
> bring peace and blessing to my community
> send rain so we are free of drought
> protect us from natural disasters
> elevate wise leaders to power in my city
> bring godly leaders to power in my state
> raise up godly men and women to lead my nation
> help righteous politicians to be elected
> heal serious situations in my state and country

reveal works of evil so they can be destroyed

expose criminals so they can be caught and imprisoned

bring an end to all gang activities

bring kidnappers and child molesters to justice

put a stop to human trafficking

cause murderers and rapists to be caught and imprisoned

bring an end to pornography

give us a godly and wise president

surround our president with godly advisors

expose corruption in government

protect our military men and women

raise up righteous judges in the courts

bring an end to wars and civil strife

destroy corruption and bias in the media

bring down evil leaders of nations

keep us safe from all acts of terrorism

cause our economy to flourish

help the unemployed to find work

place godly educators in positions of influence

pour out Your Spirit on the people of this country

Other: _____

_____

_____

Don't think for a moment that because you are only one person your prayers don't matter in this world. Let me assure you, your prayers make a big difference. If one intercessor in the Bible could have avoided a national disaster and saved a nation, what might God do through *your* prayers? Besides, there are often many of us praying about the same things, and there is tremendous power in praying together with others. Just because we are not all in the same room, church, city, state, or country at the same time, doesn't mean our prayers don't count. Every prayer you pray adds something to what God is doing or wants to do. And every prayer you pray brings greater confusion to the enemy.

Eight Things to Remember About Praying for the World Around Me

Even though things seem to be getting worse, I can't stop praying.

"Evil men and impostors will grow worse and worse, deceiving and being deceived. But you must continue in the things which you have learned and been assured of, knowing from whom you have learned them" (2 Timothy 3:13-14).

No matter how bad things get in the world, God is still in control.

"The LORD is high above all nations, His glory above the heavens. Who is like the LORD our God, who dwells on high, who humbles Himself to behold the things that are in the heavens and in the earth?" (Psalm 113:4-6).

No matter how the nations are shaken, the kingdom of God cannot be shaken.

"Since we are receiving a kingdom which cannot be shaken, let us have grace, by which we may serve God acceptably with reverence and godly fear. For our God is a consuming fire" (Hebrews 12:28-29).

I must pursue my enemies in prayer until I see them all completely destroyed.

"I have pursued my enemies and destroyed them; neither did I turn back again till they were destroyed. And I have destroyed them and wounded them, so that they could not rise; they have fallen under my feet. For You have armed me with strength for the battle; You have subdued under me those who rose against me" (2 Samuel 22:38-40).

When I sense the darkness of the world encroaching upon my life, I can pray and expect the joy of the Lord to give me strength to rise above anything that opposes me.

"You are my lamp, O LORD; the LORD shall enlighten my darkness. For by You I can run against a troop; by my God I can leap over a wall" (2 Samuel 22:29-30).

No matter how great the opposition I see to the things of God, I know He is far greater and I can have great hope and confidence in that truth.

"What then shall we say to these things? If God is for us, who can be against us?" (Romans 8:31).

My prayers lay the foundation for the pursuit of peace.

"Let us pursue the things which make for peace and the things by which one may edify another" (Romans 14:19).

God hears my prayers when I pray for the demise of evildoers.

"The eyes of the Lord are on the righteous, and His ears are open to their prayers; but the face of the LORD is against those who do evil" (1 Peter 3:12).

You may feel that you have enough to pray about with all that is going on in your own life, but praying for the world affects you too. The world today is in extremely serious trouble—far more than most people even realize. We can't afford to not pray. If you don't know what to pray about, just watch the news. You'll find more than enough things to lift up to God in just one news program. There is so much God wants to do in our world, but He is waiting for people like you and me to step in and intercede. Let's do what God wants and pray every day in some way about the world around us.

PRAYER POWER

Lord, I ask that You would help me to have faith that is strong enough to make a difference when I pray for situations and people in the world around me. Teach me how to effectively intercede. Bring to my mind everything You want me to pray about specifically.

I pray that You would pour out Your Spirit on my neighborhood of _____ , my city of _____ , my state of _____ , and my country of _____ . Draw more people to You. Open their eyes to the truth of Your Word.

I pray that You would pour out Your Spirit on my congressmen and senators, especially _____
_____
I pray for our president, _____
Cause him to serve only Your purposes. Elevate godly people into positions of leadership. Make these men and women to be people of integrity, honesty, wisdom, and discernment.

Expose evil people and evil acts. Set us free from the evils of murder, stealing, corruption, pornography, child molestation, crime, and violence. The things I see happening around me that are the most troubling are

_____

_____

_____

The things I pray You would do with regard to this are

_____

_____

_____

Lord, I pray that You would pour out Your Spirit on other countries of the world. I especially pray Your hand of protection and blessing upon Israel and for the peace of Jerusalem, as You have instructed us to do in Your Word. The other country I especially want to pray for today is _____ . I pray for the leader of that country, _____ . I pray he (she) will come to know and serve You.

The country I believe is the greatest threat to world peace is _____ . I pray You would remove all evil leaders from that country and replace them with righteous leaders. The country with the greatest struggle for its people right now is _____ . Set them free to know You and Your blessings.

You have said, "When a man's ways please the LORD, He makes even his enemies to be at peace with him" (Proverbs 16:7). I pray that in my nation we would become people who please You so that we can have peace, even with our enemies. Enable us to be a country at peace and not at war. Enable us to stay strong enough militarily to stand up to aggressive and threatening enemies. Wherever our troops are in harm's way, I pray You would protect them and give them success.

In Jesus' name I pray.

WORD POWER

I exhort first of all that supplications, prayers, intercessions, and giving of thanks be made for all men, for kings and all who are in authority, that we may lead a quiet and peaceable life in all godliness and reverence. For this is good and acceptable in the sight of God our Savior, who desires all men to be saved and to come to the knowledge of the truth.

1 TIMOTHY 2:1-4

Ask of Me, and I will give You the nations for Your inheritance, and the ends of the earth for Your possession.

PSALM 2:8

See, I have this day set you over the nations and over the kingdoms, to root out and to pull down, to destroy and to throw down, to build and to plant.

JEREMIAH 1:10

The eyes of the LORD run to and fro throughout the whole earth, to show Himself strong on behalf of those whose heart is loyal to Him.

2 CHRONICLES 16:9

Be still, and know that I am God; I will be exalted among the nations, I will be exalted in the earth!

PSALM 46:10

You shall seek them and not find them—those who contended with you. Those who war against you shall be as nothing, as a nonexistent thing. For I, the LORD your God, will hold your right hand, saying to you, "Fear not, I will help you."

ISAIAH 41:12-13

So shall they fear the name of the LORD from the west, and His glory from the rising of the sun; when the enemy comes in like a flood, the Spirit of the Lord will lift up a standard against him.

ISAIAH 59:19

ASK FOR GOD'S WILL
TO BE DONE

The Bible says we should pray according to God's will. But how do we know if our prayers are lining up with His will? The only way to be sure is to have a bottom line in your prayer that says, "Lord, in all that I have prayed and asked for, I pray most of all that Your will be done." The Bible says, "This is the confidence that we have in Him, that if we ask anything according to His will, He hears us. And if we know that He hears us, whatever we ask, we know that we have the petitions that we have asked of Him" (1 John 5:14-15). That should be reason enough for anyone to desire God's will for their life.

Every day you can ask God for what *you* want, but you should also say that above all you want what *He* wants. Jesus prayed for what He wanted, but He still prayed for

God's will to be fulfilled. He said, "Father, if it is Your will, take this cup away from Me; nevertheless not My will, but Yours, be done" (Luke 22:42). It seems that if anyone could always get what he wanted, it would be Jesus. But then He ultimately *did* get what He wanted, because what He wanted more than anything was God's will to be done. So we should pray as He did, "Not my will, but Yours, Lord, be done in my life."

Twenty Ways I Can Pray for God's Will to Be Done in My Life

"Lord, I pray that Your will be done in…"

> my marriage
>
> the lives of my children and grandchildren
>
> the lives of my mother, father, brothers, and sisters
>
> the lives of my in-laws
>
> the work I do
>
> my workplace
>
> my coworkers' lives
>
> my finances
>
> my thoughts and actions
>
> my relationships
>
> the decisions I make
>
> my health

my habits
the direction of my life
the way I spend my time
the company I keep
which church I attend
the way I pray
how I help others
every aspect of my life

God's will can be known. And we will find our greatest peace, contentment, fulfillment, and happiness when we are in the will of God. When you want to know what *God's will is* about a specific thing, ask Him to reveal it to you. When you have to make a decision and you still don't know what God's will is in the matter, then do what you know is *always* God's will. Doing that will help you to better understand the will of God in other areas. Read the list below and do those things, and you will see what I mean.

Six Things That Are Always God's Will for Me to Do

It is always God's will for me to give thanks to Him.
   "In everything give thanks; for this is the will of God in Christ Jesus for you" (1 Thessalonians 5:18).

It is always God's will for me to keep praying about everything.

"Pray without ceasing" (1 Thessalonians 5:17).

It is always God's will for me to love Him with all my heart, soul, mind, and strength.

"You shall love the Lord your God with all your heart, with all your soul, with all your mind, and with all your strength" (Mark 12:30).

It is always God's will for me to love other people.

"He answered and said, "'You shall love the LORD your God with all your heart, with all your soul, with all your strength, and with all your mind," and "your neighbor as yourself"'" (Luke 10:27).

It is always God's will for me to obey His laws.

"Why do you call Me 'Lord, Lord,' and not do the things which I say?" (Luke 6:46).

It is always God's will for me to worship and praise Him.

"By Him [Jesus] let us continually offer the sacrifice of praise to God, that is, the fruit of our lips, giving thanks to His name" (Hebrews 13:15).

When you worship God, He penetrates and softens your heart and pours into you a fresh infilling of His Holy Spirit. The more you worship Him, the more open you become to hearing His voice leading you. When that happens, even if you were being drawn toward something that wasn't God's will, your heart and mind would be touched by the Holy Spirit and turned in the right direction.

The way to make sure you are always doing the right thing is to ask God for wisdom about everything you do. "If any of you lacks wisdom, let him ask of God, who gives to all liberally and without reproach, and it will be given to him" (James 1:5). Ask Him for revelation. The Bible says, "Do not be unwise, but understand what the will of the Lord is" (Ephesians 5:17). We should not take a chance on making an unwise decision before we know what the Holy Spirit is leading us to do.

PRAYER POWER

Lord, I thank You that You can be known and that You want to reveal Your will to me. I submit myself and my life to You and ask You to reveal to me all I need to know today. Help me to hear Your voice saying, "This is the way, walk in it" (Isaiah 30:21). I pray that Your will be done in every aspect of my life.

Fill me with the knowledge of Your will. Give me wisdom and spiritual understanding (Colossians 1:9). Help me to live my life in a way that is pleasing to You. Help me to say, as wholeheartedly as Jesus said, "Not My will, but

Yours, be done" (Luke 22:42). Your will is more important to me than my own wants and desires.

Help me to know what Your will is in the decisions I make about where I should go and what I should do and who I am with. I ask, specifically, that You would reveal Your will to me about _____

_____

Lord, show me if I am doing anything that is outside of Your perfect will for my life. Help me to stay on the path You have for me. Help me to "stand perfect and complete" in all Your will (Colossians 4:12). Direct my steps, for I know I cannot find my way without You (Jeremiah 10:23). Only *You* know the way I should go. Help me to not live in the lust of my flesh but for Your will only (1 Peter 4:2). I know that only by living in Your will can I move into all You have for me.

In Jesus' name I pray.

WORD POWER

Your ears shall hear a word behind you, saying, "This is the way, walk in it," whenever you turn to the right hand or whenever you turn to the left.

ISAIAH 30:21

ANSWERS TO PRAYER

Seek God's Protection and Covering
 My Body...Home...Business...
 Family...Finances...Reputation

Tell God The Desires Of Your Heart
 Career...Finances...Relationships...
 Family...Opportunities...Accomplishments

Pray for the People in Your Life
 Family...Friends...Coworkers...
 Pastors...Neighbors...Acquaintances

Intercede for the World Around You
 Community...State...Nation...
 President...Other Countries...World Leaders

Ask for God's Will to Be Done
 Family...Work...Decisions...
 Finances...Relationships...Life

Condensed Version of the 10 Areas of Prayer Focus

Worship and Praise God for Who He Is
    Heavenly Father...Savior...Healer...
    Holy Spirit...Deliverer...Provider

Declare God to Be Lord over Your Life
    Relationships...Finances...Decisions...
    Work...Habits...Future

Invite God to Be in Charge of Your Day
    Work...Relationships...Decisions...
    Accomplishments...Choices...Meetings

Submit Your Body, Heart, and Mind to God
    Good Health...Less Stress...Clear Mind...
    No Anxiety...Complete Forgiveness...Great Joy

Confess Any Sin of Thought or Action
    Ungodly Thoughts...Wrong Words...Pride...
    Discontentment...Lack of Faith...Untruthfulness

The world is passing away, and the lust of it; but
he who does the will of God abides forever.

1 John 2:17

It is God who works in you both to will
and to do for His good pleasure.

Philippians 2:13

*Rejoice always, pray without ceasing, in
everything give thanks; for this is the
will of God in Christ Jesus for you.*

1 Thessalonians 5:16-18

*Not everyone who says to Me, "Lord, Lord,"
shall enter the kingdom of heaven, but he
who does the will of My Father in heaven.*

Matthew 7:21

*You have need of endurance, so that after you have
done the will of God, you may receive the promise.*

Hebrews 10:36

*Do not be conformed to this world, but
be transformed by the renewing of your
mind, that you may prove what is that good
and acceptable and perfect will of God.*

Romans 12:2

*For this reason we also, since the day we heard
it, do not cease to pray for you, and to ask that
you may be filled with the knowledge of His
will in all wisdom and spiritual understanding;
that you may walk worthy of the Lord, fully
pleasing Him, being fruitful in every good work
and increasing in the knowledge of God.*

Colossians 1:9-10

Ask for God's Will to Be Done